Letts

KS2 Success

Age 10-11

Mental arithmetic

Practice workbook

Paul Broadbent

About this book

Mental arithmetic

Mental arithmetic involves carrying out calculations and working with numbers in your head, without the help of a calculator or computer. It is an important part of your child's education in maths and will help them to manage everyday situations in later life. This book will help your child to solve increasingly difficult problems in their head and at greater speed. It provides the opportunity to learn, practise and check progress in a wide range of mental arithmetic skills, such as addition, subtraction, multiplication, division and working with fractions, decimals and percentages. This book will also aid preparation for the **Key Stage 2 mathematics** test.

Features of the book

Learn and revise – explains and refreshes mental arithmetic skills and strategies.

Practice activities – a variety of tasks to see how well your child has grasped each skill.

Mental arithmetic tests – 20 questions which test and reinforce your child's understanding of the preceding topics.

Speed tests and *Progress charts* – the one-minute tests challenge your child to carry out mental calculations at increasing speed and the progress charts enable them to record their results.

Key facts – a summary of key points that your child should learn by heart and memorise.

Answers are in a pull-out booklet at the centre of the book.

Mental arithmetic tips

- Cooking with your child provides opportunities to use measures – reading scales, converting between units and calculating with amounts.

- Look at prices and compare amounts when shopping. Use receipts to find differences between prices.

- Play board games, such as a simplified version of *Monopoly*, and dice games, such as *Yahtzee*, taking opportunities to add and subtract numbers and money.

- Addition and subtraction facts to 20 and the multiplication tables are basic key facts that your child will need to know so that they can solve problems with bigger numbers. Regularly practise these facts – you could write them on sticky notes around the house for your child to see or answer.

- Short, regular practice to build confidence is better than spending too long on an activity so that boredom creeps in. Keep each session to 20–30 minutes.

Contents

Numbers and place value

Learn and revise

One more than 999 999 is 1 million.

1 million is written as 1 000 000.

Use this chart to help you read numbers greater than 1 million.

Millions			Thousands			Ones		
hundreds	tens	units	hundreds	tens	units	hundreds	tens	units
		6	8	4	3	9	1	8

6 843 918 is read as 6 **million** 843 **thousand** 918.

6 000 000 + 800 000 + 40 000 + 3000 + 900 + 10 + 8 = 6 843 918

Practice activities

1. Read these and write each as a number.

   a) six million four hundred thousand nine hundred and twenty-six

   _____

   b) nine million two hundred and eighteen thousand and seventy-four

   _____

   c) two million one hundred thousand   _____

   d) three million two hundred and ninety thousand five hundred and ninety-one

   _____

   e) one million four hundred thousand two hundred and twelve _____

   f) four million one thousand three hundred and ninety   _____

   g) seven million two thousand and eight   _____

   h) one million four hundred thousand two hundred and sixty _____

2. Write each of these numbers as words.

   a) 6 785 141 _____

   _____

   b) 1 510 930 _____

   _____

   c) 4 890 081 _____

   _____

3. Circle the correct digit in each number to match the value.

   Example: 2 0 6 7 ③ 9 5   three hundred

   a) 2 9 6 9 9 2 1   nine hundred thousand

   b) 7 2 2 4 0 2 5   twenty thousand

   c) 3 3 6 3 2 8 0   three million

   d) 8 5 5 0 1 5 9 7   five hundred thousand

4. Here are the approximate populations of some of the largest cities in the world. Write the cities in order of population, starting with the largest.

Cairo (Egypt) 15 837 460   **London (UK) 12 412 330**

Mexico City (Mexico) 22 843 550   **Mumbai (India) 19 463 950**

Moscow (Russia) 14 432 190   **New York (USA) 22 310 740**

Shanghai (China) 16 708 510   **Tokyo (Japan) 35 521 740**

City	Country	Population

Negative numbers

Learn and revise

All whole numbers are called **integers**. Integers can be positive or negative. Zero is an integer.

Remember the following:

- When you move left on a number line, numbers get smaller.
- When you move right on a number line, numbers get larger.

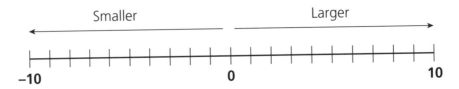

Smaller   Larger

$\leqslant$ means 'less than or equals' $\geqslant$ means 'more than or equals'

Practice activities

1. What number does each arrow point to?

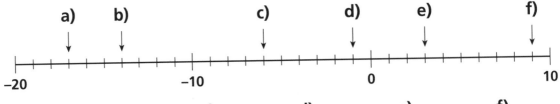

a) ____   b) ____   c) ____   d) ____   e) ____   f) ____

2. Look at the number line above. What is the difference between:

   a)   a) and d)? ____   b)   c) and e)? ____

   c)   b) and f)? ____   d)   e) and b)? ____

3. Write these temperatures in order, starting with the lowest.

   18°C   −13°C   −14°C   0°C   3°C   −5°C

   ____ ____ ____ ____ ____ ____

   lowest

4. What is the difference in temperature between these pairs of thermometers?

a)

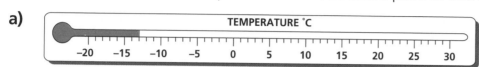

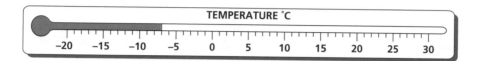

_____

b)

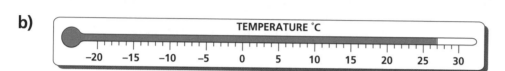

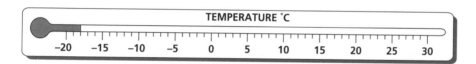

_____

c)

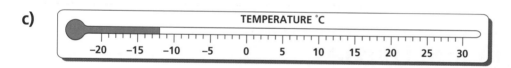

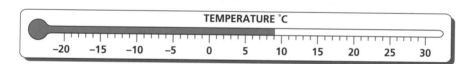

_____

5. Rashid was trying to roll a marble on to a target line of exactly 1 metre. He recorded each attempt in centimetres above or below his target.

1st	2nd	3rd	4th	5th	6th	7th	8th
+6	+1	−4	−7	−2	0	+2	−3

a) What was the length of his longest roll? _____

b) What was the length of his shortest roll? _____

c) On which attempt did he land on the target line? _____

d) On which attempt did he roll 97 cm? _____

e) How would he have recorded a roll of 94 cm?

_____

Order of operations

If a calculation involves brackets, then the calculation must be done in the following order:

	Example:
Brackets	$5 \times (3 + 8) - 2$ — *Brackets first,*
Division	$= 5 \times 11 - 2$ — *no division, so now multiply,*
Multiplication	$= 55 - 2$ — *no addition, so now subtract*
Addition	$= 53$
Subtraction	

Compare these to see how important brackets are:

$26 - (5 + 12) = 9$

$(26 - 5) + 12 = 33$

$(12 \div 4) + 2 = 5$

$12 \div (4 + 2) = 2$

Practice activities

1. Answer these.

   a) $(27 - 13) + 4$ = _____

   b) $54 - (17 + 12)$ = _____

   c) $(23 - 15) \times 2$ = _____

   d) $52 - (28 - 19)$ = _____

   e) $3 \times (29 - 18)$ = _____

   f) $(12 + 36) \div 2$ = _____

   g) $(48 + 6) - (12 \times 3)$ = _____

   h) $(9 \times 4) \div (22 - 16)$ = _____

2. Write in brackets to make these true.

   a) $5 \quad - \quad 3 \quad \times \quad 4 \quad + \quad 2 \quad = \quad 12$

   b) $15 \quad + \quad 21 \quad \div \quad 7 \quad - \quad 8 \quad = \quad 10$

   c) $9 \quad \div \quad 3 \quad + \quad 6 \quad - \quad 5 \quad = \quad 4$

   d) $2 \quad \times \quad 4 \quad + \quad 2 \quad \times \quad 4 \quad = \quad 48$

   e) $5 \quad + \quad 10 \quad - \quad 18 \quad \div \quad 9 \quad = \quad 13$

3. Write the missing numbers.

a) ($\boxed{} \times 4) - 1 = 11$

b) $10 - (\boxed{} \times 3) = 4$

c) $(4 \times 2) + (\boxed{} \times 3) = 17$

d) $(\boxed{} \times 5) - (5 \times 4) = 10$

e) $12 \div (\boxed{} \times 2) = 2$

4. Use only the numbers 2, 4, 5, 6 and 8 and any operation (+, −, ×, ÷).

Can you find different ways to make the numbers 1 to 20? Try to use brackets for each one.

Example: $(5 + 8) - (2 \times 6) = 1$

1 ⟶	11 ⟶	
2 ⟶	12 ⟶	
3 ⟶	13 ⟶	
4 ⟶	14 ⟶	
5 ⟶	15 ⟶	
6 ⟶	16 ⟶	
7 ⟶	17 ⟶	
8 ⟶	18 ⟶	
9 ⟶	19 ⟶	
10 ⟶	20 ⟶	

Mental arithmetic test 1

1. $(24 \div 3) + 9 =$ _____

2. Write six million two hundred and ten thousand and fifty as a number.

   _____

3. $45 - (8 + 7) =$ _____

4. Write < or > to make this true.

   $925\,059$ _____ $2\,905\,522$

5. $(34 + 8) \div 6 =$ _____

6. Circle the lowest temperature and underline the highest temperature.

   $-12°C$ $-2°C$ $-20°C$

      $21°C$ $-1°C$

7. $60 \div (3 \times 4) =$ _____

8. Write the value of the underlined digit.

   7 683 141

   _____

9. $(5 \times 9) - (36 - 12) =$ _____

10. Circle the largest and underline the smallest number.

    $8\,136\,470$ $8\,134\,607$

    $8\,317\,019$ $8\,731\,097$ $8\,130\,974$

11. Circle the digit with a value of **nine hundred**.

    $9\,0\,9\,9\,9\,9\,0$

12. $6 \times (13 - 5) =$ _____

13. Write < or > to make this true.

    10 _____ -11

14. $(7 \times 3) + 54 =$ _____

15. Write four million eight thousand one hundred and sixty as a number.

    _____

16. $25 - (32 \div 4) =$ _____

17. $(40 - 28) \times (27 \div 3) =$ _____

    Use this number line in 18–20.

18. Write the number at each arrow.

    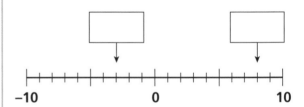

19. What is the difference between -4 and -7?

    _____

20. What is the difference between -5 and 2?

    _____

Score   /20

10

Mental arithmetic test 2

1. $(28 ÷ 7) × 20 =$ _____

2. Circle the digit with a value of **thirty thousand**.

   5 3 3 3 3 5 3

3. $9 + (11 − 3) =$ _____

4. Write two million one hundred and six thousand and ten as a number.

   _____

5. $(40 × 5) − 160 =$ _____

Use this number line in 6–8.

6. Write the number at each arrow.

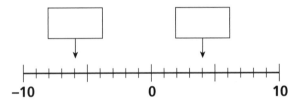

7. What is the difference between −1 and −6?

   _____

8. What is the difference between −8 and 5?

   _____

9. Write the missing number.

   $54 ÷ (2 +$ _____ $) = 6$

10. Write < or > to make this true.

    −15 _____ 5

11. Write five million forty-one thousand six hundred as a number.

    _____

12. $(6 × 6) ÷ (15 − 6) =$ _____

13. $(40 − 32) × 7 =$ _____

14. Circle the largest and underline the smallest number.

    4 667 452   4 674 250

    6 204 765   6 240 076   4 720 554

15. Write the missing number.

    $90 + (5 ×$ _____ $) = 120$

16. Write the value of the underlined digit.

    9 782 485

    _____

17. $8 × (4 + 5) =$ _____

18. Circle the lowest temperature and underline the highest temperature.

    14°C   4°C   −19°C

            −3°C   −9°C

19. Write < or > to make this true.

    1 518 032 _____ 581 083

20. $(35 + 25) − (40 ÷ 8) =$ _____

Score   /20

11

Addition and subtraction

Learn and revise

When you add two numbers mentally, you can add to one of the numbers, as long as you subtract the same amount from the other number.

Example:

$$68 + 73 \longrightarrow \begin{array}{c} 68 + 2 = \mathbf{70} \\ 73 - 2 = \mathbf{71} \end{array} \longrightarrow 70 + 71 = 141$$

When you subtract two numbers mentally, you can add to or subtract from one of the numbers, as long as you do the same to the other number.

Example:

$$113 - 87 \longrightarrow \begin{array}{c} 113 + 3 = \mathbf{116} \\ 87 + 3 = \mathbf{90} \end{array} \longrightarrow 116 - 90 = 26$$

Practice activities

1. Add these mentally. Use the method shown if it helps.

    a) $59 + 86$ = ____ + ____ = ____

    b) $67 + 48$ = ____ + ____ = ____

    c) $83 + 98$ = ____ + ____ = ____

    d) $107 + 76$ = ____ + ____ = ____

    e) $119 + 104$ = ____ + ____ = ____

    f) $154 + 191$ = ____ + ____ = ____

2. Subtract these mentally. Use the method shown if it helps.

a) 83 – 57 = _____ – _____ = _____

b) 76 – 48 = _____ – _____ = _____

c) 94 – 76 = _____ – _____ = _____

d) 125 – 49 = _____ – _____ = _____

e) 154 – 87 = _____ – _____ = _____

f) 143 – 105 = _____ – _____ = _____

3. Investigate this problem, called 'Kaprekar's Constant'.

- Take any three digits that are not all identical.

- Rearrange the digits to form the largest and smallest three-digit numbers possible.

- Subtract the smaller number from the larger.

- Take the answer and repeat the above process, making the smallest and largest possible numbers and finding the difference.

- Repeat this again and again.

What number do you end up with? _____

Example:

4   3   6

The largest three-digit number is 643 and the smallest is 346.

$643 - 346 = 297$

$972 - 279 = 693$

$963 - 369 = 594$

$954 - 459 = 495$

$954 - 459 = 495$

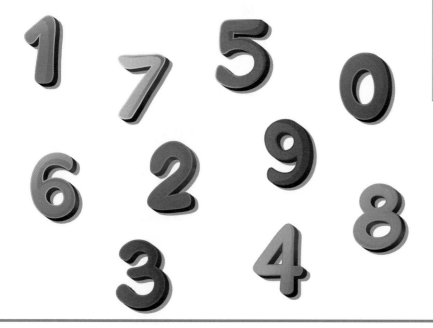

Multiplication

Learn and revise

When you multiply tenths by a whole number, change the tenth to a whole number (by multiplying by 10), multiply the two numbers and then divide the answer by 10.

Example: What is 0.8×3?

$$0.8 \times 10 = 8$$
$$8 \times 3 = 24$$
$$24 \div 10 = 2.4$$
$$\text{So } 0.8 \times 3 = 2.4$$

When you multiply decimals greater than 1, break the decimal number into the whole number and tenth. Multiply each part then add the two numbers together.

Example: What is 1.7×5?

$$1.7 \times 5 = (1 \times 5) + (0.7 \times 5)$$
$$= \quad 5 \quad + \quad 3.5$$
$$= 8.5$$

Practice activities

1. Answer these.

    a) 8×5 = _____

    0.8×5 = _____

    b) 3×7 = _____

    0.3×7 = _____

    c) 9×4 = _____

    0.9×4 = _____

    d) 7×6 = _____

    0.7×6 = _____

    e) 8×8 = _____

    0.8×8 = _____

    f) 7×9 = _____

    0.7×9 = _____

    g) 7×7 = _____

    0.7×7 = _____

    h) 9×5 = _____

    0.9×5 = _____

2. Complete these.

   a) $4.3 \times 5 = \quad (4 \times 5) \quad + \quad (0.3 \times 5)$

   $\qquad\qquad = \underline{\quad\quad} \quad + \quad \underline{\quad\quad}$

   $\qquad\qquad = \underline{\qquad\qquad\quad}$

   b) $7.5 \times 8 = (\underline{\quad} \times \underline{\quad}) + (\underline{\quad} \times \underline{\quad})$

   $\qquad\qquad = \underline{\quad\quad} \quad + \quad \underline{\quad\quad}$

   $\qquad\qquad = \underline{\qquad\qquad\quad}$

   c) $8.6 \times 9 = (\underline{\quad} \times \underline{\quad}) + (\underline{\quad} \times \underline{\quad})$

   $\qquad\qquad = \underline{\quad\quad} \quad + \quad \underline{\quad\quad}$

   $\qquad\qquad = \underline{\qquad\qquad\quad}$

   d) $5.9 \times 3 = (\underline{\quad} \times \underline{\quad}) + (\underline{\quad} \times \underline{\quad})$

   $\qquad\qquad = \underline{\quad\quad} \quad + \quad \underline{\quad\quad}$

   $\qquad\qquad = \underline{\qquad\qquad\quad}$

   e) $6.2 \times 7 = (\underline{\quad} \times \underline{\quad}) + (\underline{\quad} \times \underline{\quad})$

   $\qquad\qquad = \underline{\quad\quad} \quad + \quad \underline{\quad\quad}$

   $\qquad\qquad = \underline{\qquad\qquad\quad}$

3. Use the digits 3, 6 and 8.

$$\boxed{3} \quad \boxed{6} \quad \boxed{8}$$

Arrange them like this to make different multiplications:

$$\boxed{} \cdot \boxed{} \times \boxed{} =$$

   a) What is the largest answer you can make? $\underline{\qquad\qquad}$

   b) What is the smallest answer you can make? $\underline{\qquad\qquad}$

   c) What answer is the nearest to 30? $\underline{\qquad\qquad}$

Division

Learn and revise

Learn and use these rules of divisibility.

A whole number is divisible by, or can be divided exactly by:	
2 if the last digit is even, e.g. 34, 78, 136, 5100	**6** if it is even and the sum of its digits is divisible by 3, e.g. 816 (8 + 1 + 6 = 15) 714 (7 + 1 + 4 = 12)
3 if the sum of its digits can be divided by 3, e.g. 261 (2 + 6 + 1 = 9) 1005 (1 + 0 + 0 + 5 = 6)	**8** if the last three digits can be divided by 8, e.g. 7264 (264 ÷ 8 = 33) 19 432 (432 ÷ 8 = 54)
4 if the last two digits can be divided by 4, e.g. 508 (08 ÷ 4 = 2) 364 (64 ÷ 4 = 16) 9320 (20 ÷ 4 = 5)	**9** if the sum of its digits is divisible by 9, e.g. 675 (6 + 7 + 5 = 18) 2043 (2 + 0 + 4 + 3 = 9)
5 if the last digit is 0 or 5, e.g. 530, 105, 485	**10** if the last digit is 0, e.g. 580, 2630, 48 900

Practice activities

1. Each of these numbers is exactly divisible by 9.

The last digit is missing. Write the missing digits.

a) 525__ **b)** 259__ **c)** 842__

d) 736__ **e)** 704__ **f)** 199__

2. Write the numbers 2, 3, 4, 5, 6, 8, 9 or 10 in the correct spaces. Use the rules of divisibility to find the answers.

a) 96 is divisible by _____, _____, _____, _____ and _____.

b) 81 is divisible by _____ and _____.

c) 170 is divisible by _____, _____ and _____.

d) 156 is divisible by _____, _____, _____ and _____.

e) 1680 is divisible by _____, _____, _____, _____, _____, _____ and _____.

f) 4050 is divisible by _____, _____, _____, _____, _____ and _____.

3. Write these numbers in the correct sections of the Venn diagram.

| 2130 | 2004 | 5317 | 2790 | 3294 |

| 3700 | 5193 | 6219 | 6154 | 4815 |

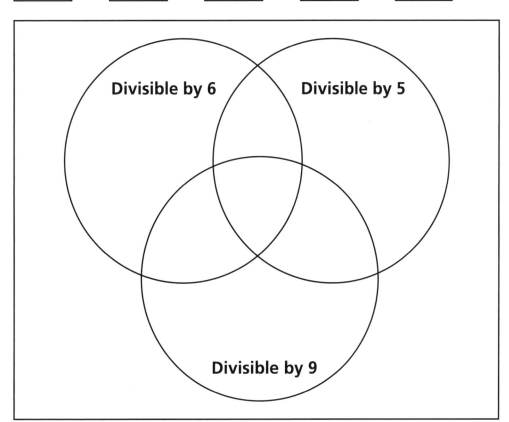

Divisible by 6

Divisible by 5

Divisible by 9

Mental arithmetic test 3

1. Multiply these.

$7 \times 5 =$ _____

$0.7 \times 5 =$ _____

2. $45 + 46 =$ _____

3. Circle the number that is exactly divisible by 9.

859   384   726

123   432

4. $238 - 93 =$ _____

5. A cinema ticket costs £2.70. What is the total cost of four tickets?

£ _____

6. Will 6 divide exactly into 2634?

Circle your answer.

Yes / No

7. $0.9 \times 2 =$ _____

8. Write the last digit of this number to make it exactly divisible by 8.

135___

9. $72 - 15 =$ _____

10. $183 + 52 =$ _____

11. $579 - 36 =$ _____

12. $10.4 \times 3 =$ _____

13. Circle the numbers that will divide exactly into 234.

5   8

6   9

14. $127 + 19 =$ _____

15. $0.8 \times 9 =$ _____

16. What is 44p less than 81p?

_____ p

17. $7.5 \times 8 =$ _____

18. Which two numbers between 2052 and 2059 are divisible by 3?

_____ and _____

19. A café serves 163 teas and 74 coffees in one day. How many teas and coffees did they serve altogether?

_____

20. $6.7 \times 6 =$ _____

Score   /20

Mental arithmetic test 4

1. $206 + 36 =$ _____

2. Tom is 15 cm shorter than his mum. His mum is 164 cm tall. How tall is Tom?

   _____ cm

3. Multiply these.

   $4 \times 8 =$ _____

   $0.4 \times 8 =$ _____

4. Write two numbers between 37 and 48 that are divisible by 5.

   _____ and _____

5. $0.3 \times 5 =$ _____

6. Circle the numbers that will divide exactly into 272.

   4   6   9

        5   8

7. $24 + 57 =$ _____

8. Will 8 divide exactly into 1284?

   Circle your answer.

   Yes / No

9. A boat ride costs £1.80 per person. What is the total cost for three people?

   £ _____

10. $190 - 21 =$ _____

11. $81 - 49 =$ _____

12. $0.9 \times 9 =$ _____

13. Circle the number that is exactly divisible by 6.

    459   274   962

         708   513

14. $135 + 91 =$ _____

15. Which two numbers between 6245 and 6253 are exactly divisible by 4?

    _____ and _____

16. $2.4 \times 6 =$ _____

17. I have 27p in my pocket and 57p in my purse. How much have I got altogether?

    _____ p

18. Write the last digit of this number to make it exactly divisible by 9.

    475__

19. $257 - 83 =$ _____

20. $7.6 \times 9 =$ _____

Score   /20

19

Multiples and factors

Learn and revise

Make sure you know the difference between **multiples** and **factors**.

Multiples

Multiples of any number can be divided exactly by that number. For example:

- 8, 12, 16, 20 and 24 are all multiples of 4.
- 12, 18, 24, 30 and 36 are all multiples of 6.

12 and 24 are **common multiples** of 4 and 6.

The **lowest common multiple** (LCM) of 4 and 6 is 12.

Factors

Factors are whole numbers that will divide exactly into other whole numbers. For example:

- The factors of 32 are (1, 32), (2, 16), (4, 8).
- The factors of 18 are (1, 18), (2, 9), (3, 6).

Numbers which are factors of two or more numbers are called **common factors**.

The common factors of 18 and 32 are 1 and 2.

The **highest common factor** (HCF) of 18 and 32 is 2.

Practice activities

1. Find all the common multiples up to 99 for each pair of numbers.

   a) 3 and 5 _____

   b) 6 and 10 _____

   c) 4 and 9 _____

   d) 2 and 5 _____

2. Write the lowest common multiple for each pair of numbers in practice activity 1.

   a) ____   b) ____

   c) ____   d) ____

Multiples and factors

3. What is the lowest common multiple for each of these?

   a) 6 and 8   ____   b) 9 and 5   ____

   c) 2, 3 and 5 ____   d) 4, 9 and 6 ____

   e) 6, 4 and 5 ____   f) 8, 3 and 2 ____

4. Write the factors of these numbers in pairs.

   a) 48 _____

   b) 27 _____

   c) 45 _____

   d) 36 _____

   e) 30 _____

   f) 42 _____

5. Look at your answers for practice activity 4. Use them to help you find the **common factors** for each of these.

   a) Common factors of 30 and 42   _____

   b) Common factors of 27 and 45   _____

   c) Common factors of 36 and 42   _____

   d) Common factors of 42 and 48   _____

   e) Common factors of 30 and 45   _____

   f) Common factors of 27, 36 and 45 _____

   g) Common factors of 36, 42 and 48 _____

   Now circle the **highest common factor** in each of your answers.

Squares and primes

Learn and revise

Make sure you know what **square numbers** and **prime numbers** are.

Square numbers

The numbers 1, 4, 9 and 16 are examples of **square numbers**. Square numbers are found when two identical whole numbers are multiplied together, e.g.

3 squared = 9

4 squared = 16

$3^2 = 9$

$4^2 = 16$

Prime numbers

If a number only has two factors, itself and 1, then it is a **prime number**. For example, 17 is a prime number because it can only be divided exactly by 1 and 17.

The number 1 is not a prime number because it only has one factor – itself.

Practice activities

1. Answer these.

   a) $3 \times 3 = 3^2 =$ _____

   b) $10 \times 10 = 10^2 =$ _____

   c) $4 \times 4 = 4^2 =$ _____

   d) $6 \times 6 = 6^2$ = _____

   e) 2^2 = _____

   f) 12^2 = _____

   g) 5^2 = _____

   h) 7^2 = _____

   i) 8^2 = _____

   j) 1^2 = _____

   k) 9^2 = _____

   l) 11^2 = _____

2. Investigate the number of factors for each of the square numbers in practice activity 1.

   Complete this sentence:

   Square numbers always have an _____ number of factors.

3. Eratosthenes was a Greek mathematician who lived from 275 BC to 195 BC. He discovered a method of finding prime numbers of less than 100.

To use his method, follow the stages under the grid below:

1	2	3	4	5	6	7	8	9	10
11	12	13	14	15	16	17	18	19	20
21	22	23	24	25	26	27	28	29	30
31	32	33	34	35	36	37	38	39	40
41	42	43	44	45	46	47	48	49	50
51	52	53	54	55	56	57	58	59	60
61	62	63	64	65	66	67	68	69	70
71	72	73	74	75	76	77	78	79	80
81	82	83	84	85	86	87	88	89	90
91	92	93	94	95	96	97	98	99	100

a) On this number grid, cross out numbers using different colours:

- Cross out 1.
- Cross out all the multiples of 2, but not 2.
- Cross out all the multiples of 3, but not 3.
- Cross out all the multiples of 5, but not 5.
- Cross out all the multiples of 7, but not 7.

b) Write down all the numbers that you have not crossed out. If you have done it correctly, this will be a list of all the prime numbers to 100.

_____

_____

_____

c) What do you notice about the factors of each of the numbers you have listed in part **b)**?

_____

Patterns and relationships

Learn and revise

You can often find the pattern or rule in a sequence by looking at the difference between the numbers.

Example: What is the next number in this sequence?

| 12 | 7 | 2 | -3 | -8 | _____ |

Each number is 5 less than the previous one, so the next number is -13.

The rule is 'subtract 5'.

A **formula** (plural is **formulae**) uses letters or words to give a rule.

Example: What is the rule for the relationship between A and B for each pair of numbers?

A	0	1	2	3	4	5	n
B	1	3	5	7	9	?	?

To work out B, you can double A then add 1: $B = 2A + 1$

So for n (or any number), the formula is $2n + 1$. You can use this to find any number in the sequence, so the 12th number is:

$$2 \times 12 + 1 = 25$$

Practice activities

1. Write the next two numbers and the rule for each sequence.

a) | -9 | -3 | 3 | 9 | 15 | _____ _____ | the rule is _____

b) | -20 | -9 | 2 | 13 | 24 | _____ _____ | the rule is _____

c) | 26 | 17 | 8 | -1 | -10 | _____ _____ | the rule is _____

d) | 255 | 205 | 155 | 105 | 55 | _____ _____ | the rule is _____

e) | 3.45 | 3.65 | 3.85 | 4.05 | 4.25 | _____ _____ | the rule is _____

2. Write the value of B for each of these when A is 5.

Choose the correct rule for each relationship between A and B.

a)

A	0	1	2	3	4	5	n
B	0	2	4	6	8		?

$3n - 1$ $n + 1$ $2n$ $2n - 1$

b)

A	0	1	2	3	4	5	n
B	3	5	7	9	11		?

$4n$ $n + 3$ $3n + 1$ $2n + 3$

c)

A	0	1	2	3	4	5	n
B	−4	−3	−2	−1	0		?

$n - 2$ $5 - n$ $n - 4$ $2n - 5$

d)

A	0	1	2	3	4	5	n
B	−2	1	4	7	10		?

$2n - 4$ $2n + 1$ $3n - 2$ $3 - 2n$

3. For each of the sequences in practice activity 2, what is the value of B if A is 30?

a) ____   **b)** ____

c) ____   **d)** ____

Mental arithmetic test 5

1. Write the missing pair of factors for 32.

   $32 \rightarrow$ (1, 32) (2, 16) (_____, _____)

2. Circle the numbers that are multiples of both 2 and 9.

   27   64   36

        72   45

3. $5^2 = $ _____

4. Circle the prime number.

   39   43   33

        21   15

5. What is the lowest common multiple of 4 and 7?

   _____

6. Write the missing factor for 50.

   1, 2, 5, 10 , _____, 50

   Look at these numbers for 7–8.

   | 36   24   12   _____ |

7. Write the rule for this sequence of numbers.

   The rule is _____

8. What would be the next number in this sequence?

   _____

9. Circle the numbers that are multiples of both 6 and 8.

   42   72   48

        56   36

10. $6^2 = $ _____

11. What are the common factors of 42 and 21?

    _____

    Look at these numbers for 12–13.

    | 5.5   5.9   6.3   6.7   _____ |

12. Write the rule for this sequence of numbers.

    The rule is _____

13. What would be the next number in this sequence?

    _____

14. $8^2 = $ _____

15. What is the next prime number after 19?

    _____

    Look at this chart for 16–17.

A	0	1	2	3	4	5	n
B	0	3	6	9	12	_____	?

16. Write in the chart the value of B when A is 5.

17. Circle the correct rule for the relationship between A and B.

    $n + 3$ $3n$ $2n + 1$ $4n - 1$

18. $11^2 = $ _____

19. What are the common factors of 18, 9 and 27?

    _____

20. What is the lowest common multiple of 4, 3 and 6?

    _____

Score   /20

1. Circle the numbers that are multiples of both 6 and 4.

60   54   28

42   36

2. Write the missing factor for 45.

1, 3, 5, _____, 15, 45

3. Circle the prime number.

9   25   15

17   27

4. $7^2 =$ _____

5. What is the lowest common multiple of 5 and 3?

_____

6. Write the next prime number after 23.

_____

7. Write the missing pair of factors for 42.

$42 \rightarrow$ (1, 42) (2, 21) (3, 14) (_____, _____)

8. Circle the numbers that are multiples of both 7 and 3.

84   56   24   42   35

Look at these numbers for 9–10.

| 7 | 2 | –3 | –8 | _____ |

9. Write the rule for this sequence of numbers.

The rule is _____

10. What would be the next number in this sequence?

_____

11. $9^2 =$ _____

Look at this chart for 12–13.

A	0	1	2	3	4	5	n
B	1	3	5	7	9	_____	?

12. Write in the chart the value of B when A is 5.

13. Circle the correct rule for the relationship between A and B.

$2n + 1$ $n + 2$ $2n$ $2n - 1$

14. What are the common factors of 28 and 42?

_____

15. $10^2 =$ _____

Look at these numbers for 16–17.

| 396   426   456   486   _____ |

16. Write the rule for this sequence of numbers.

The rule is _____

17. What would be the next number in this sequence?

_____

18. $12^2 =$ _____

19. What is the lowest common multiple of 2, 5 and 4?

_____

20. What are the common factors of 12, 20 and 16?

_____

Score   /20

27

Comparing fractions

It is easier to compare fractions if they have the same denominator. If the denominators are not the same, you need to change them to equivalent fractions with a **common denominator**. To do this, you need to know the **lowest common multiple** for each denominator.

Example: Which is the larger fraction, $\frac{3}{5}$ or $\frac{3}{4}$?

First, change them to equivalent fractions.

The lowest common multiple of 5 and 4 is 20.

$$\overset{\times\,4}{\frac{3}{5}} = \underset{\times\,4}{\frac{12}{20}} \qquad\qquad \overset{\times\,5}{\frac{3}{4}} = \underset{\times\,5}{\frac{15}{20}}$$

$\frac{15}{20} > \frac{12}{20}$ so $\frac{3}{4}$ is greater than $\frac{3}{5}$.

Practice activities

1. Complete the pairs of equivalent fractions.

a) $\frac{2}{3} = \frac{\Box}{9}$

b) $\frac{5}{8} = \frac{10}{\Box}$

c) $\frac{\Box}{5} = \frac{2}{10}$

d) $\frac{1}{\Box} = \frac{3}{9}$

e) $\frac{\Box}{6} = \frac{30}{36}$

f) $\frac{4}{5} = \frac{\Box}{20}$

g) $\frac{1}{9} = \frac{6}{\Box}$

h) $\frac{7}{\Box} = \frac{35}{50}$

i) $\frac{3}{11} = \frac{\Box}{33}$

j) $\frac{7}{10} = \frac{56}{\Box}$

k) $\frac{\Box}{9} = \frac{24}{27}$

l) $\frac{6}{\Box} = \frac{36}{42}$

2. Write <, > or = between each pair of fractions.

Remember to change them to equivalent fractions.

a) $\frac{2}{3}$ ☐ $\frac{5}{6}$ **b)** $\frac{4}{7}$ ☐ $\frac{3}{4}$

c) $\frac{1}{3}$ ☐ $\frac{2}{5}$ **d)** $\frac{3}{8}$ ☐ $\frac{2}{5}$

e) $\frac{4}{5}$ ☐ $\frac{3}{4}$ **f)** $\frac{5}{8}$ ☐ $\frac{3}{10}$

g) $\frac{7}{12}$ ☐ $\frac{1}{2}$ **h)** $\frac{3}{5}$ ☐ $\frac{2}{3}$

3. Answer these problems.

a) A market trader has the same number of melons and pineapples to sell. After an hour, $\frac{5}{8}$ of his melons are sold and $\frac{7}{12}$ of his pineapples are sold. Which fruit has sold more?

_____

b) James and Lizzie each had a bag of sweets with the same number of sweets in each bag. James has $\frac{7}{10}$ of his sweets left and Lizzie has $\frac{5}{6}$ of her sweets left. Who has eaten more sweets?

_____

c) When United played City in the league, the stadium was $\frac{3}{5}$ full. When they played each other in the cup, later in the season, the stadium was $\frac{5}{8}$ full. Which match had a bigger crowd – league or cup?

_____

d) In a library there are fiction, non-fiction and poetry books. $\frac{7}{15}$ of the books are non-fiction and $\frac{5}{12}$ of them are fiction. Are there more fiction or non-fiction books?

_____

Fractions of amounts

Learn and revise

Finding fractions of quantities is very similar to dividing amounts.

Example: What is $\frac{2}{3}$ of 15?

$\frac{1}{3}$ of 15 = 15 ÷ 3 = 5

$\frac{2}{3}$ of 15 = 5 × 2 = 10 ⟵ *If the numerator is more than 1, divide the quantity by the denominator and then multiply by the numerator.*

Sometimes fractions of amounts leave fraction remainders.

Example: What is $\frac{1}{4}$ of 11?

$\frac{1}{4}$ of 11 = 2 remainder 3 $\frac{1}{4}$ of this remainder = $\frac{3}{4}$

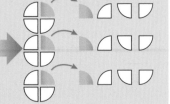
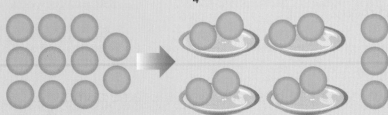

$\frac{1}{4}$ of 11 = $2\frac{3}{4}$

Practice activities

1. Complete each of these.

a) $\frac{2}{3}$ of...	b) $\frac{4}{5}$ of...	c) $\frac{3}{4}$ of...	d) $\frac{7}{10}$ of...
27 = ____	40 = ____	36 = ____	90 = ____
84 = ____	35 = ____	92 = ____	30 = ____
120 = ____	105 = ____	180 = ____	110 = ____
90 = ____	250 = ____	108 = ____	70 = ____

Answers

Pages 4–5

1. a) 6400926   b) 9218074
    c) 2100000   d) 3290591
    e) 1400212   f) 4001390
    g) 7002008   h) 1400260

2. a) six million seven hundred and eighty-five thousand one hundred and forty-one
    b) one million five hundred and ten thousand nine hundred and thirty
    c) four million eight hundred and ninety thousand and eighty-one

3. a) 2⓪69921
    b) 7 2②4 025
    c) ③363280
    d) 85⑤01597

4.

City	Country	Population
Tokyo	Japan	35521740
Mexico City	Mexico	22843550
New York	USA	22310740
Mumbai	India	19463950
Shanghai	China	16708510
Cairo	Egypt	15837460
Moscow	Russia	14432190
London	UK	12412330

Pages 6–7

1. a) −17   b) −14   c) −6
    d) −1   e) 3   f) 9

2. a) 16   b) 9
    c) 23   d) 17

3. −14°C, −13°C, −5°C, 0°C, 3°C, 18°C

4. a) 6°   b) 45°   c) 21°

5. a) 1m 6cm (or 106cm)   b) 93cm (or 0.93m)
    c) 6th attempt   d) 8th attempt
    e) 6 below the target (−6)

Pages 8–9

1. a) 18   b) 25
    c) 16   d) 43
    e) 33   f) 24
    g) 18   h) 6

2. a) $(5 − 3) \times (4 + 2) = 12$
    b) $15 + (21 \div 7) − 8 = 10$
    c) $(9 \div 3) + (6 − 5) = 4$
    d) $2 \times (4 + 2) \times 4 = 48$
    e) $(5 + 10) − (18 \div 9) = 13$

3. a) 3   b) 2   c) 3
    d) 6   e) 3

4. There are many possible solutions. Check each calculation gives each number from 1–20 as the answer.

Page 10

1. 17   2. 6210050
3. 30   4. <
5. 7
6. −20° C 21°C
7. 5
8. six hundred thousand (or 600000)
9. 21
10. 8731097, 8130974
11. 9 0 9 9 ⑨ 9 0

12. 48   13. >
14. 75   15. 4008160
16. 17   17. 108
18. −3, 8   19. 3
20. 7

Page 11

1. 80   2. 5 3 ③ 3 3 5 3
3. 17   4. 2106010
5. 40   6. −6, 4
7. 5   8. 13
9. 7   10. <
11. 5041600   12. 4
13. 56
14. 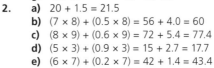 6240076, 4667452
15. 6
16. nine million (or 9000000)
17. 72
18. 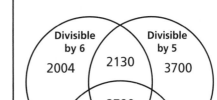 −19° C 14°C
19. >   20. 55

Pages 12–13

1. a) 145   b) 115
    c) 181   d) 183
    e) 223   f) 345

2. a) 26   b) 28
    c) 18   d) 76
    e) 67   f) 38

3. 495

Pages 14–15

1. a) 40, 4.0   b) 21, 2.1
    c) 36, 3.6   d) 42, 4.2
    e) 64, 6.4   f) 63, 6.3
    g) 49, 4.9   h) 45, 4.5

2. a) $20 + 1.5 = 21.5$
    b) $(7 \times 8) + (0.5 \times 8) = 56 + 4.0 = 60$
    c) $(8 \times 9) + (0.6 \times 9) = 72 + 5.4 = 77.4$
    d) $(5 \times 3) + (0.9 \times 3) = 15 + 2.7 = 17.7$
    e) $(6 \times 7) + (0.2 \times 7) = 42 + 1.4 = 43.4$

3. a) 50.4   b) 20.4   c) 28.8

Pages 16–17

1. a) 6   b) 2
    c) 4   d) 2
    e) 7   f) 8

2. a) 2, 3, 4, 6 and 8
    b) 3 and 9
    c) 2, 5 and 10
    d) 2, 3, 4 and 6
    e) 2, 3, 4, 5, 6, 8 and 10
    f) 2, 3, 5, 6, 9 and 10

3.

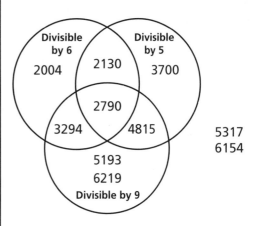

Divisible by 6: 2004
Divisible by 5: 3700
Divisible by 9: 5193, 6219
2130
2790
3294
4815
5317, 6154

1

Answers

Page 18

1.	35, 3.5	**2.**	91
3.	432	**4.**	145
5.	£10.80	**6.**	Yes
7.	1.8	**8.**	2
9.	57	**10.**	235
11.	543	**12.**	31.2
13.	6, 9	**14.**	146
15.	7.2	**16.**	37p
17.	60	**18.**	2055 and 2058
19.	237	**20.**	40.2

Page 19

1.	242	**2.**	149 cm
3.	32, 3.2	**4.**	40 and 45
5.	1.5	**6.**	4, 8
7.	81	**8.**	No
9.	£5.40	**10.**	169
11.	32	**12.**	8.1
13.	708	**14.**	226
15.	6248 and 6252	**16.**	14.4
17.	84p	**18.**	2
19.	174	**20.**	68.4

Pages 20–21

1.
  a) 15, 30, 45, 60, 75, 90
  b) 30, 60, 90
  c) 36, 72
  d) 10, 20, 30, 40, 50, 60, 70, 80, 90

2.
  a) 15   b) 30
  c) 36   d) 10

3.
  a) 24   b) 45
  c) 30   d) 36
  e) 60   f) 24

4.
  a) (1, 48) (2, 24) (3, 16) (4, 12) (6, 8)
  b) (1, 27) (3, 9)
  c) (1, 45) (3, 15) (5, 9)
  d) (1, 36) (2, 18) (3, 12) (4, 9) (6, 6)
  e) (1, 30) (2, 15) (3, 10) (5, 6)
  f) (1, 42) (2, 21) (3, 14) (6, 7)

5.
  a) 1, 2, 3, ⑥   b) 1, 3, ⑨
  c) 1, 2, 3, ⑥   d) 1, 2, 3, ⑥
  e) 1, 3, 5, ⑮   f) 1, 3, ⑨
  g) 1, 2, 3, ⑥

Pages 22–23

1.
  a) 9   b) 100
  c) 16   d) 36
  e) 4   f) 144
  g) 25   h) 49
  i) 64   j) 1
  k) 81   l) 121

2. odd

3.
  a) Check all the numbers have been crossed out except those listed in **b)**.
  b) 2, 3, 5, 7, 11, 13, 17, 19, 23, 29, 31, 37, 41, 43, 47, 53, 59, 61, 67, 71, 73, 79, 83, 89, 97
  c) Each number only has two factors, 1 and itself.

Pages 24–25

1.
  a) 21, 27   the rule is +6
  b) 35, 46   the rule is +11
  c) −19, −28   the rule is −9
  d) 5, −45   the rule is −50
  e) 4.45, 4.65   the rule is +0.2

2.
  a) 10, $2n$
  b) 13, $2n + 3$
  c) 1, $n - 4$
  d) 13, $3n - 2$

3.
  a) 60
  b) 63
  c) 26
  d) 88

Page 26

1.	(4, 8)	**2.**	72, 36
3.	25	**4.**	43
5.	28	**6.**	25
7.	−12	**8.**	0
9.	72, 48	**10.**	36
11.	1, 3, 7, 21	**12.**	+0.4
13.	7.1	**14.**	64
15.	23	**16.**	15
17.	$3n$	**18.**	121
19.	1, 3, 9	**20.**	12

Page 27

1.	60, 36	**2.**	9
3.	17	**4.**	49
5.	15	**6.**	29
7.	(6, 7)	**8.**	84, 42
9.	−5	**10.**	−13
11.	81	**12.**	11
13.	$2n + 1$	**14.**	1, 2, 7, 14
15.	100	**16.**	+30
17.	516	**18.**	144
19.	20	**20.**	1, 2, 4

Pages 28–29

1.
  a) 6   b) 16
  c) 1   d) 3
  e) 5   f) 16
  g) 54   h) 10
  i) 9   j) 80
  k) 8   l) 7

2.
  a) < b) < c) < d) <
  e) > f) > g) > h) <

3.
  a) melons   b) James
  c) cup   d) non-fiction

Pages 30–31

1.
  a) 18, 56, 80, 60
  b) 32, 28, 84, 200
  c) 27, 69, 135, 81
  d) 63, 21, 77, 49

2.
  a) $2\frac{2}{3}$
  b) $2\frac{2}{5}$
  c) $2\frac{1}{2}$ (or $2\frac{2}{4}$)
  d) $6\frac{1}{2}$
  e) $1\frac{1}{2}$
  f) $3\frac{1}{3}$

3.
  a) £12
  b) 18
  c) 160 m
  d) 0.9 kg (or 900 g)
  e) 20

4.
  a) $\frac{3}{4}$ of 4.4 kg
  b) $\frac{7}{10}$ of 4 kg
  c) $\frac{3}{5}$ of 4.5 kg
  d) $\frac{3}{4}$ of 1.2 kg

Pages 32–33

1.
  a) $2\frac{7}{8}$ b) $1\frac{1}{10}$
  c) $1\frac{11}{15}$ d) $3\frac{19}{20}$
  e) $1\frac{3}{20}$ f) $4\frac{39}{40}$

2.
  a) $2\frac{1}{2}$ b) $3\frac{1}{9}$
  c) $1\frac{1}{5}$ d) $2\frac{13}{24}$
  e) $\frac{13}{20}$ f) $1\frac{1}{20}$

3.
  a) $2\frac{1}{20}$ b) $3\frac{7}{30}$
  c) $3\frac{27}{40}$ d) $3\frac{13}{15}$
  e) $1\frac{1}{4}$ f) $3\frac{3}{5}$

4. $\frac{1}{3} + \frac{1}{6} = \frac{1}{2}$
$\frac{3}{10} + \frac{1}{5} = \frac{1}{2}$
$\frac{3}{8} + \frac{1}{4} = \frac{5}{8}$

Page 34
1. $\frac{6}{15}, \frac{6}{16}$
2. Tuesday
3. 60
4. <
5. $3\frac{1}{8}$
6. $\frac{3}{4}$ of 4.8 km
7. $4\frac{39}{40}$
8. 14
9. $\frac{25}{35}, \frac{12}{16}$
10. $\frac{5}{9} < \frac{4}{7} < \frac{2}{3}$
11. $\frac{3}{10}$ of 5 kg
12. $2\frac{3}{20}$
13. $1\frac{1}{6}$
14. 27
15. 36
16. $4\frac{4}{5}$
17. >
18. $3\frac{43}{60}$
19. $\frac{3}{10}$ m
20. $\frac{9}{10}$ of the cake

Page 35
1. 120
2. $3\frac{17}{30}$
3. $\frac{10}{14}, \frac{24}{30}$
4. $\frac{3}{4} < \frac{7}{9} < \frac{5}{6}$
5. $3\frac{1}{6}$
6. 45
7. $2\frac{11}{40}$
8. >
9. $\frac{2}{3}$ of 1.8 kg
10. blue
11. $\frac{16}{40}, \frac{15}{24}$
12. 4
13. $5\frac{5}{7}$
14. 44
15. >
16. $\frac{7}{8}$ of the pizza
17. 13
18. $\frac{5}{6}$ of 5.4 m
19. $1\frac{11}{45}$
20. $4\frac{7}{20}$

Pages 36–37
1. a) 0.7   b) 0.9
   c) 0.4   d) 0.8
   e) 0.5   f) 0.75
   g) 0.45   h) 0.08
   i) 0.33   j) 0.09
2. a) $\frac{1}{2}$ b) $\frac{3}{10}$
   c) $\frac{7}{10}$ d) $\frac{4}{5}$
   e) $\frac{2}{5}$ f) $\frac{21}{50}$
   g) $\frac{4}{25}$ h) $\frac{39}{50}$
   i) $\frac{17}{20}$ j) $\frac{2}{25}$
3. a) $4\frac{2}{10} = 4.2$ b) $9\frac{4}{10} = 9.4$
   c) $3\frac{8}{10} = 3.8$ d) $11\frac{6}{10} = 11.6$
   e) $4\frac{5}{10} = 4.5$ f) $3\frac{4}{100} = 3.04$
   g) $5\frac{78}{100} = 5.78$ h) $10\frac{6}{100} = 10.06$
   i) $6\frac{35}{100} = 6.35$ j) $2\frac{5}{100} = 2.05$
4. a) $\frac{7}{100}, \frac{3}{10}, \frac{37}{100}, \frac{7}{10}$
   b) $\frac{41}{100}, \frac{1}{2}, \frac{3}{5}, \frac{7}{10}$
   c) $\frac{1}{50}, \frac{2}{25}, \frac{14}{50}, \frac{4}{5}$
   d) $\frac{29}{50}, \frac{18}{25}, \frac{3}{4}, \frac{4}{5}$

Pages 38–39
1. a) $\frac{1}{2} = 0.5 = 50\%$
   b) $\frac{1}{4} = 0.25 = 25\%$
   c) $\frac{1}{5} = 0.2 = 20\%$
   d) $\frac{2}{5} = 0.4 = 40\%$
   e) $\frac{17}{50} = 0.34 = 34\%$
   f) $\frac{7}{10} = 0.7 = 70\%$
   g) $\frac{7}{100} = 0.07 = 7\%$
   h) $\frac{11}{25} = 0.44 = 44\%$
2. a) $\frac{4}{5}$ b) $\frac{13}{25}$
   c) $\frac{3}{5}$ d) $\frac{17}{50}$
   e) $\frac{7}{20}$ f) $\frac{13}{50}$
   g) $\frac{1}{50}$ h) $\frac{49}{50}$
3. a) 70%   b) 75%
   c) 80%   d) 90%
   e) 60%   f) 79%
4. a) Beth
   b) $\frac{45}{50}, \frac{4}{5}, \frac{79}{100}, \frac{15}{20}, \frac{7}{10}, \frac{15}{25}$
5. a) $\frac{3}{4}$ blue, $\frac{3}{20}$ red, $\frac{1}{20}$ white, $\frac{1}{20}$ yellow
   b) $\frac{3}{5}$ blue, $\frac{3}{10}$ yellow, $\frac{2}{25}$ white, $\frac{1}{50}$ black
   c) $\frac{11}{20}$ yellow, $\frac{1}{4}$ red, $\frac{9}{50}$ white, $\frac{1}{50}$ black

Pages 40–41
1.

		What is?			
	10% of …	20% of …	5% of …	50% of …	25% of …
£20	£2	£4	£1	£10	£5
£60	£6	£12	£3	£30	£15
£50	£5	£10	£2.50	£25	£12.50
£24	£2.40	£4.80	£1.20	£12	£6

2. a) £3, £9   b) £7, £28
   c) £2.50, £7.50   d) £0.80, £0.40
   e) £0.60, £1.20   f) £4, £48
3. a) Amount off: £4; Sale price: £36
   b) Amount off: £6; Sale price: £54
   c) Amount off: £14; Sale price: £56
   d) Amount off: £10; Sale price: £15
   e) Amount off: £4; Sale price: £76

Page 42
1. $\frac{3}{10}, \frac{4}{5}$
2. $\boxed{\frac{72}{100}}, \frac{2}{10}$
3. 0.2, 0.6
4. 0.5, 50%
5. $\frac{2}{5}, \frac{13}{50}$
6. $6\frac{8}{10} = 6.8, 7\frac{5}{10} = 7.5$
7. 0.09, 9%
8. £3
9. $\frac{17}{20}, \frac{1}{4}$
10. £40
11. 0.25, 0.7
12. 0.4, 40%
13. £4.50
14. $\frac{9}{25}, \frac{57}{100}$
15. £4
16. $\frac{1}{20}, \frac{4}{25}$
17. 0.3, 0.09
18. $\boxed{\frac{4}{5}}, \frac{8}{100}$
19. 0.55, 55%
20. $1\frac{18}{100} = 1.18, 3\frac{55}{100} = 3.55$

Page 43
1. 0.8, 0.4
2. $\frac{9}{10}, \frac{3}{5}$
3. $\boxed{\frac{9}{10}}, \frac{9}{100}$
4. 0.25, 25%
5. £27
6. $\frac{1}{5}, \frac{29}{50}$
7. £12
8. 0.42, 0.6
9. 0.07, 7%
10. $2\frac{6}{10} = 2.6, 4\frac{2}{10} = 4.2$
11. 0.75, 75%
12. $4\frac{6}{100} = 4.06, 10\frac{4}{100} = 10.04$
13. $\frac{1}{25}, \frac{7}{25}$
14. 0.9, 0.03
15. 0.38, 38%
16. $\frac{7}{20}, \frac{3}{4}$
17. 0.48, 48%
18. $\boxed{\frac{2}{5}}, \frac{4}{100}$
19. £3
20. $\frac{9}{100}, \frac{6}{25}$

Pages 44–45
1. a) $\frac{1}{2}$ (or $\frac{3}{6}$)   b) $\frac{1}{2}$ (or $\frac{4}{8}$)
   c) $\frac{7}{10}$ d) $\frac{2}{5}$
   e) $\frac{3}{4}$ (or $\frac{6}{8}$)
2. a) 1 : 1   b) 1 : 1   c) 7 : 3
   d) 2 : 3   e) 3 : 1
3. a) 18   b) 3 : 1   c) 24
4. a) 300 g flour, 150 g butter, 100 g sugar, 50 g chocolate chips
   b) 450 g flour, 225 g butter, 150 g sugar, 75 g chocolate chips

Pages 46–47
1. a) $\triangle = 7$ b) $\blacklozenge = 15$
   c) $\blacklozenge = 2$ d) $\blacklozenge = 32$
   e) $y = 24$ f) $b = 5$
   g) $n = 6$ h) $t = 3$
2. a) 4   b) 5
   c) 4   d) 9
   e) 3   f) 10
3. a) 31   b) 49
   c) 160   d) 5
   e) 2   f) 54

Answers

4. a) [x = 1, y = 24] [x = 2, y = 12] [x = 3, y = 8] [x = 4, y = 6]
        [x = 6, y = 4] [x = 8, y = 3] [x = 12, y = 2] [x = 24, y = 1]
    b) x = 8, y = 3

Pages 48–49
1. a) 90, 80, 80, 80, 70, 70, 60, 50, 50
    b) 70   c) 80   d) 70
2. a) 140 cm   b) 140 cm   c) 150 cm
3. Median: 29 seconds; Mode: 28 seconds; Mean: 30 seconds
4. Median: 10 cm; Mode: 10 cm; Mean: 10 cm

Page 50
1. 18   2. 100 g
3. 200 g   4. 16
5. 7   6. 28
7. 30   8. 29
9. $\frac{1}{2}$ 10. 1 : 1
11. $\frac{3}{4}$ 12. 6
13. 170 cm   14. 170 cm
15. 175 cm   16. 5
17. 48   18. 3
19. 17   20. 16

Page 51
1. $\frac{1}{3}$ 2. 1 : 2
3. 6   4. 10
5. 32 g   6. 34 g
7. 34 g   8. 20
9. 2   10. 86
11. 6   12. 1 : 3
13. 8   14. 12°C
15. 12°C   16. 12°C
17. 3   18. 65
19. 3   20. mode

Page 52
1. 120   2. 27
3. 30   4. 0.7
5. 90   6. 31
7. 55   8. 26
9. 80   10. 52
11. 900   12. 33
13. 3000   14. $1\frac{3}{5}$
15. 140   16. 28
17. 950   18. 1.4
19. 9   20. 25
21. 1100   22. 31
23. 7   24. 14
25. 1.3   26. 0.2
27. $\frac{2}{3}$ 28. 8
29. 90   30. 6

31. 680   32. 250
33. $3\frac{1}{5}$ 34. 25
35. 5   36. 330
37. 220   38. 0.3
39. 42   40. 40

Page 54
1. 72   2. 56
3. 9   4. 7
5. 64   6. 84
7. 6   8. 9
9. 800   10. 7
11. 25   12. 2400
13. 21   14. 11
15. 1.4   16. 5
17. 0.18   18. 8
19. 7   20. 72
21. 30   22. 140
23. 121   24. 60
25. 345   26. 132
27. 270   28. 49
29. 1.98   30. 6
31. 6   32. 810
33. 23   34. 36
35. 60   36. 50
37. 1600   38. 2.4
39. 630   40. 30

Page 56
1. 28   2. 140
3. 108   4. 370
5. 60   6. 400
7. 4   8. 110
9. 72   10. 11
11. 15   12. 96
13. 0.9   14. 1.3
15. 1000   16. 5
17. 100   18. 80
19. 40   20. 400
21. 180   22. 90
23. 20   24. 17
25. 16   26. 31
27. 880   28. 3500
29. 1.5   30. 38
31. 12   32. 132
33. 19   34. 160
35. 8   36. 20
37. 20   38. 80
39. 180   40. 144

Published by Letts Educational
An imprint of HarperCollins*Publishers* Ltd
1 London Bridge Street
London SE1 9GF

ISBN 9781844198634

Text © 2015 Paul Broadbent

Design © 2015 Letts Educational, an imprint of
HarperCollins*Publishers* Ltd

The author asserts his moral right to be identified as the
author of this work.

2. Answer these, writing each remainder as a fraction.

a)

$\frac{1}{3}$ of 8 = _____

b)

$\frac{1}{5}$ of 12 = _____

c)

$\frac{1}{4}$ of 10 = _____

d)

$\frac{1}{2}$ of 13 = _____

e)

$\frac{1}{8}$ of 12 = _____

f)

$\frac{1}{3}$ of 10 = _____

3. Answer these.

a) What is three-quarters of £16? £_____

b) There are 27 children in a class and two-thirds are girls.

How many are girls? _____

c) What is four-fifths of 200 metres? _____ m

d) Three-fifths of the ingredients in a cake is flour. If the total weight of the cake is 1.5 kg, what is the weight of the flour used?

_____

e) I am thinking of a number. Three-quarters of the number is 15.

What is the number I am thinking of? _____

4. Which of these is the heavier weight in each pair?

a) $\frac{2}{3}$ of 3.9 kg or $\frac{3}{4}$ of 4.4 kg

_____

b) $\frac{7}{10}$ of 4 kg or $\frac{2}{3}$ of 3600 g

_____

c) $\frac{3}{5}$ of 4.5 kg or $\frac{7}{10}$ of 2400 g

_____

d) $\frac{3}{4}$ of 1.2 kg or $\frac{2}{5}$ of 1.5 kg

_____

Fraction calculations

Learn and revise

Fractions with different denominators are called **unlike fractions**. To add or subtract unlike fractions, you change them to like fractions by looking for equivalent fractions with a common denominator.

Follow these steps:

- Find equivalent fractions with a common denominator.
- Add the numerators and write the numerator over the common denominator.
- Simplify the fraction if needed.

Example: Add $\frac{1}{4}$ and $1\frac{2}{5}$.

Common denominator is 20.

$\frac{5}{20} + 1\frac{8}{20} = 1\frac{13}{20}$

Example: Subtract $\frac{1}{6}$ from $1\frac{2}{3}$.

Common denominator is 6.

$1\frac{4}{6} - \frac{1}{6} = 1\frac{3}{6} = 1\frac{1}{2}$

Practice activities

1. Find the common denominator for the fractions in each addition. Write the answers in their simplest form.

   a) $\frac{1}{8} + 2\frac{3}{4}$ = _____

   b) $\frac{4}{5} + \frac{3}{10}$ = _____

   c) $1\frac{2}{3} + \frac{1}{15}$ = _____

   d) $2\frac{7}{10} + 1\frac{1}{4}$ = _____

   e) $\frac{3}{4} + \frac{2}{5}$ = _____

   f) $4\frac{3}{5} + \frac{3}{8}$ = _____

2. Find a common denominator and subtract these. Simplify your answers if needed.

    a) $2\frac{4}{5} - \frac{3}{10}$ = _____

    b) $3\frac{2}{3} - \frac{5}{9}$ = _____

    c) $1\frac{1}{2} - \frac{3}{10}$ = _____

    d) $2\frac{7}{8} - \frac{1}{3}$ = _____

    e) $\frac{4}{5} - \frac{3}{20}$ = _____

    f) $2\frac{3}{4} - 1\frac{7}{10}$ = _____

3. Read and answer these. Simplify your answers if needed.

    a) What is $2\frac{3}{4}$ less than $4\frac{4}{5}$? _____

    b) Subtract $3\frac{7}{15}$ from $6\frac{7}{10}$. _____

    c) What is the difference between $2\frac{1}{5}$ and $5\frac{7}{8}$? _____

    d) What is $4\frac{1}{5}$ take away $\frac{1}{3}$? _____

    e) What is $5\frac{7}{20}$ subtract $4\frac{1}{10}$? _____

    f) What is the difference between $4\frac{1}{2}$ and $\frac{9}{10}$? _____

4. Complete these calculations by using each of the digits 1 to 6 to fill in the boxes.

| 1 | 2 | 3 | 4 | 5 | 6 |

    $\dfrac{\square}{3} + \dfrac{1}{\square} = \dfrac{1}{2}$ $\dfrac{\square}{10} + \dfrac{1}{5} = \dfrac{1}{\square}$ $\dfrac{3}{8} + \dfrac{1}{\square} = \dfrac{\square}{8}$

Mental arithmetic test 7

1. Complete these equivalent fractions.

   $\frac{2}{5} = \frac{\boxed{}}{15}$ $\frac{3}{8} = \frac{6}{\boxed{}}$

2. Amy reads $\frac{3}{10}$ of her book on Monday and $\frac{2}{5}$ of the book on Tuesday.

   On which day did she read most?

   _____

3. $\frac{3}{10}$ of 200 = _____

4. Write < or > between this pair of fractions.

   $\frac{1}{4}$ _____ $\frac{4}{7}$

5. Answer this, writing the remainder as a fraction.

   $\frac{1}{8}$ of 25 = _____

6. Circle the longer distance.

   $\frac{1}{2}$ of 5.6 km $\frac{3}{4}$ of 4.8 km

7. $\frac{3}{5} + 4\frac{3}{8} =$ _____

8. What is two-thirds of 21?

   _____

9. Complete these equivalent fractions.

   $\frac{5}{7} = \frac{\boxed{}}{35}$ $\frac{3}{4} = \frac{12}{\boxed{}}$

10. Write these fractions in order.

    $\frac{2}{3}$ $\frac{5}{9}$ $\frac{4}{7}$

    _____ < _____ < _____

11. Circle the heavier weight.

    $\frac{3}{10}$ of 5 kg $\frac{2}{5}$ of 3 kg

12. What is $\frac{3}{4}$ less than $2\frac{9}{10}$?

    _____

13. $2\frac{5}{6} - 1\frac{2}{3} =$ _____

14. A necklace has 36 beads and three-quarters are blue. How many beads are blue?

    _____

15. $\frac{3}{5}$ of 60 = _____

16. Answer this, writing the remainder as a fraction.

    $\frac{1}{5}$ of 24 = _____

17. Write < or > between this pair of fractions.

    $\frac{2}{3}$ _____ $\frac{3}{5}$

18. $2\frac{3}{10} + 1\frac{5}{12} =$ _____

19. Lee can throw a ball $3\frac{4}{5}$ m and Ben can throw a ball $3\frac{1}{2}$ m. How much further can Lee throw a ball than Ben?

    _____ m

20. Circle the larger slice of cake.

    $\frac{9}{10}$ of the cake $\frac{5}{6}$ of the cake

Score   **/20**

34

Mental arithmetic test 8

1. $\frac{2}{3}$ of 180 = _____

2. $\frac{1}{6} + 3\frac{2}{5}$ = _____

3. Complete these equivalent fractions.

   $\frac{5}{7} = \frac{\square}{14}$ $\qquad$ $\frac{4}{5} = \frac{24}{\square}$

4. Write these fractions in order.

   $\frac{5}{6}$ $\qquad$ $\frac{3}{4}$ $\qquad$ $\frac{7}{9}$

   _____ < _____ < _____

5. Answer this, writing the remainder as a fraction.

   $\frac{1}{6}$ of 19 = _____

6. What is three-quarters of 60?

   _____

7. $4\frac{7}{8} - 2\frac{3}{5}$ = _____

8. Write < or > between this pair of fractions.

   $\frac{1}{3}$ ____ $\frac{2}{9}$

9. Circle the heavier weight.

   $\frac{3}{4}$ of 1.2 kg $\qquad$ $\frac{2}{3}$ of 1.8 kg

10. There are two packs of balloons, one red and the other blue, each with the same number of balloons. In the red pack $\frac{1}{4}$ of the balloons are large and in the blue pack $\frac{3}{8}$ of the balloons are large.

    Which colour pack has more large balloons, red or blue?

    _____

11. Complete these equivalent fractions.

    $\frac{4}{10} = \frac{\square}{40}$ $\qquad$ $\frac{5}{8} = \frac{15}{\square}$

12. A bus had 20 passengers and one-fifth got off at the cinema. How many passengers got off the bus?

    _____

13. Answer this, writing the remainder as a fraction.

    $\frac{1}{7}$ of 40 = _____

14. $\frac{4}{5}$ of 55 = _____

15. Write < or > between this pair of fractions.

    $\frac{3}{4}$ ____ $\frac{7}{10}$

16. Circle the larger slice of pizza.

    $\frac{7}{8}$ of the pizza $\qquad$ $\frac{5}{6}$ of the pizza

17. My gran is 78 years old. My mum is half my gran's age and I am one-third of my mum's age. How many years old am I?

    _____

18. Circle the longer length.

    $\frac{5}{8}$ of 4.8 m $\qquad$ $\frac{5}{6}$ of 5.4 m

19. What is the difference between $2\frac{4}{5}$ and $1\frac{5}{9}$?

    _____

20. $1\frac{3}{5} + 2\frac{3}{4}$ = _____

Score _____ /20

35

Fractions and decimals

Learn and revise

To change fractions to decimals, change them to tenths or hundredths.

This number line is divided into tenths. They are written as common fractions and decimal fractions.

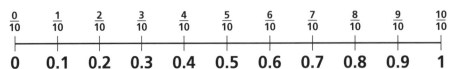

$\frac{1}{10} = 0.1$ zero point one

$\frac{2}{10} = 0.2$ zero point two

$\frac{2}{10}$ can be simplified to $\frac{1}{5}$, so $\frac{1}{5}$ is equal to 0.2

There are fractions and decimals between tenths.

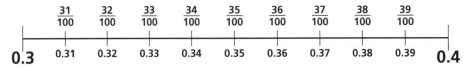

$\frac{31}{100} = 0.31$ zero point three one

$\frac{32}{100} = 0.32$ zero point three two

$\frac{32}{100}$ can be simplified to $\frac{8}{25}$, so $\frac{8}{25}$ is equal to 0.32

Practice activities

1. Write these as decimals.

     a) $\frac{7}{10} = $ _____   b) $\frac{9}{10} = $ _____

     c) $\frac{2}{5} = $ _____   d) $\frac{4}{5} = $ _____

     e) $\frac{50}{100} = $ _____   f) $\frac{75}{100} = $ _____

     g) $\frac{45}{100} = $ _____   h) $\frac{8}{100} = $ _____

     i) $\frac{33}{100} = $ _____   j) $\frac{9}{100} = $ _____

Fractions and decimals

2. Write these as fractions. Simplify them if possible.

a) 0.5 = _____   **b)** 0.3 = _____

c) 0.7 = _____   **d)** 0.8 = _____

e) 0.4 = _____   **f)** 0.42 = _____

g) 0.16 = _____   **h)** 0.78 = _____

i) 0.85 = _____   **j)** 0.08 = _____

3. Change these to tenths or hundredths and write them as decimal fractions.

a) $4\frac{1}{5}$ = _____ = _____   **b)** $9\frac{2}{5}$ = _____ = _____

c) $3\frac{4}{5}$ = _____ = _____   **d)** $11\frac{3}{5}$ = _____ = _____

e) $4\frac{1}{2}$ = _____ = _____   **f)** $3\frac{1}{25}$ = _____ = _____

g) $5\frac{39}{50}$ = _____ = _____   **h)** $10\frac{3}{50}$ = _____ = _____

i) $6\frac{7}{20}$ = _____ = _____   **j)** $2\frac{1}{20}$ = _____ = _____

4. Write each set in order, starting with the smallest.

a)

$\frac{3}{10}$	$\frac{7}{10}$	$\frac{7}{100}$	$\frac{37}{100}$

____ ____ ____ ____

smallest

b)

$\frac{1}{2}$	$\frac{3}{5}$	$\frac{7}{10}$	$\frac{41}{100}$

____ ____ ____ ____

smallest

c)

$\frac{2}{25}$	$\frac{14}{50}$	$\frac{4}{5}$	$\frac{1}{50}$

____ ____ ____ ____

smallest

d)

$\frac{4}{5}$	$\frac{29}{50}$	$\frac{18}{25}$	$\frac{3}{4}$

____ ____ ____ ____

smallest

Fractions, decimals and percentages

Learn and revise

It is easy to convert between percentages and decimals.

per cent to decimal	decimal to per cent
Divide the percentage by 100, e.g.	Multiply the decimal by 100, e.g.
40% is the same as 0.4	0.35 is the same as 35%

When you convert from fractions to percentages, you may find it easier to write the fraction as a decimal and then multiply by 100. For example, $\frac{3}{4}$ is 0.75, which is the same as 75%.

Practice activities

1. Complete these.

   a) $\dfrac{1}{\square}$ = 0.$\square$ = 50%

   b) $\dfrac{\square}{4}$ = 0.25 = ____%

   c) $\dfrac{1}{5}$ = 0.$\square$ = ____%

   d) $\dfrac{2}{\square}$ = 0.4 = ____%

   e) $\dfrac{17}{50}$ = 0.$\square$ = ____%

   f) $\dfrac{7}{\square}$ = 0.7 = ____%

   g) $\dfrac{\square}{100}$ = 0.07 = ____%

   h) $\dfrac{11}{\square}$ = 0.44 = ____%

2. Write each of these percentages as a fraction reduced to its simplest form.

   a) 80% = ____

   b) 52% = ____

   c) 60% = ____

   d) 34% = ____

   e) 35% = ____

   f) 65% = ____

   g) 2% = ____

   h) 98% = ____

Fractions, decimals and percentages

3. Change these test scores to percentages.

Name	Score	Percentage
	☐	☐
	☐	☐
	☐	☐
	☐	☐
	☐	☐
	☐	☐

a) Adam: $\frac{7}{10}$ = _____%

b) Ben: $\frac{15}{20}$ = _____%

c) Anna: $\frac{4}{5}$ = _____%

d) Beth: $\frac{45}{50}$ = _____%

e) Asif: $\frac{15}{25}$ = _____%

f) Claire: $\frac{79}{100}$ = _____%

4. Look at the results in practice activity 3.

a) Which child has the highest percentage score? _____

b) Write the test scores in order, starting with the highest.

_____ _____ _____ _____ _____ _____

highest

5. These are the percentages of colours used to mix different paints. Convert the percentages to fractions in their simplest form.

a)

75% blue = _____

15% red = _____

5% white = _____

5% yellow = _____

b)

60% blue = _____

30% yellow = _____

8% white = _____

2% black = _____

c)

55% yellow = _____

25% red = _____

18% white = _____

2% black = _____

Percentages

Learn and revise

Look at the following percentage question.

Example: What is 20% of £40?

Try these two methods to solve this type of percentage question.

Method 1	**Method 2**
Change to a fraction and work it out: $20\% = \frac{20}{100} = \frac{1}{5}$ $\frac{1}{5}$ of £40 = £40 ÷ 5 = £8	Use 10% to work it out – just divide the number by 10: 10% of £40 is £4 So, 20% of £40 is double that: £8

Practice activities

1. Complete this table.

	What is?				
	10% of …	**20% of …**	**5% of …**	**50% of…**	**25% of …**
£20	£2				
£60			£3		
£50		£10			
£24					£6

2. Write the percentages of each of these amounts.

a) £30

10% = £____

30% = £____

b) £70

10% = £____

40% = £____

c) £25

10% = £____

30% = £____

d) £8

10% = £____

5% = £____

e) £60

1% = £____

2% = £____

f) £400

1% = £____

12% = £____

3. In a sale everything is reduced in price. Write the amount taken off and the new cost of each item. Remember to subtract the percentage of the price from the original price.

a)   Was £40 ⟶ Now 10% off

Amount off: £____   Sale price: £____

b)  Was £60 ⟶ Now reduced by 10%

Amount off: £____   Sale price: £____

c)  Was £70 ⟶ 20% discount today

Amount off: £____   Sale price: £____

d)   Was £25 ⟶ Special offer 40% off

Amount off: £____   Sale price: £____

e)   Was £80 ⟶ Now reduced by 5%

Amount off: £____   Sale price: £____

Mental arithmetic test 9

1. Write these as fractions. Simplify them if possible.

    0.3 = _____   0.8 = _____

2. Circle the largest and underline the smallest fraction.

    $\frac{27}{100}$ $\frac{7}{10}$ $\frac{2}{10}$ $\frac{72}{100}$

3. Write these as decimals.

    $\frac{1}{5}$ = _____ $\frac{3}{5}$ = _____

4. $\frac{1}{2}$ = _____•_____ = _____%

5. Write these as fractions. Simplify them if possible.

    40% = _____   26% = _____

6. Change these to tenths or hundredths and write them as decimal fractions.

    $6\frac{4}{5}$ = _____ = _____

    $7\frac{1}{2}$ = _____ = _____

7. $\frac{9}{100}$ = _____•_____ = _____%

8. 5% of £60 = £ _____

9. Write these as fractions. Simplify them if possible.

    0.85 = _____   0.25 = _____

10. In a sale there is 20% off a chair at £50. What is the sale price of the chair?

    £_____

11. Write these as decimals.

    $\frac{25}{100}$ = _____ $\frac{70}{100}$ = _____

12. $\frac{2}{5}$ = _____•_____ = _____%

13. 15% of £30 = £_____

14. Write these as fractions. Simplify them if possible.

    0.36 = _____   0.57 = _____

15. 25% of £16 = £_____

16. Write these as fractions. Simplify them if possible.

    5% = _____   16% = _____

17. Write these as decimals.

    $\frac{3}{10}$ = _____ $\frac{9}{100}$ = _____

18. Circle the largest and underline the smallest fraction.

    $\frac{7}{10}$ $\frac{3}{4}$ $\frac{4}{5}$ $\frac{8}{100}$

19. $\frac{11}{20}$ = _____•_____ = _____%

20. Change these to tenths or hundredths and write them as decimal fractions.

    $1\frac{9}{50}$ = _____ = _____

    $3\frac{11}{20}$ = _____ = _____

Score   /20

42

Mental arithmetic test 10

1. Write these as decimals.

   $\frac{4}{5}$ = _____ $\frac{2}{5}$ = _____

2. Write these as fractions. Simplify them if possible.

   0.9 = _____   0.6 = _____

3. Circle the largest and underline the smallest fraction.

   $\frac{9}{10}$ $\frac{19}{100}$ $\frac{1}{10}$ $\frac{9}{100}$

4. $\frac{1}{4}$ = _____•_____ = _____%

5. In a sale there is 10% off a coat for £30. What is the sale price of the coat?

   £_____

6. Write these as fractions. Simplify them if possible.

   20% = _____   58% = _____

7. 30% of £40 = £_____

8. Write these as decimals.

   $\frac{42}{100}$ = _____ $\frac{60}{100}$ = _____

9. $\frac{7}{100}$ = _____•_____ = _____%

10. Change these to tenths or hundredths and write them as decimal fractions.

    $2\frac{3}{5}$ = _____ = _____

    $4\frac{1}{5}$ = _____ = _____

11. $\frac{75}{100}$ = _____•_____ = _____%

12. Change these to tenths or hundredths and write them as decimal fractions.

    $4\frac{3}{50}$ = _____ = _____

    $10\frac{1}{25}$ = _____ = _____

13. Write these as fractions. Simplify them if possible.

    4% = _____   28% = _____

14. Write these as decimals.

    $\frac{9}{10}$ = _____ $\frac{3}{100}$ = _____

15. $\frac{19}{50}$ = _____•_____ = _____%

16. Write these as fractions. Simplify them if possible.

    0.35 = _____   0.75 = _____

17. $\frac{12}{25}$ = _____•_____ = _____%

18. Circle the largest and underline the smallest fraction.

    $\frac{3}{10}$ $\frac{1}{4}$ $\frac{2}{5}$ $\frac{4}{100}$

19. 15% of £20 = £_____

20. Write these as fractions. Simplify them if possible.

    0.09 = _____   0.24 = _____

Score   /20

43

Ratio and proportion

Ratio compares one amount with another.

Example: What is the ratio of yellow to red tiles?

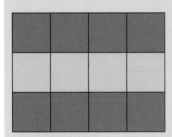

For every one yellow tile, there are two red tiles. The ratio of yellow to red is 1 to 2, written as 1 : 2.

This ratio stays the same for any number of tiles arranged in this way:

Yellow	1	2	3	4	5	6
Red	2	4	6	8	10	12

Working out the **proportion** is the same as finding the fraction of the whole amount. The proportion of yellow tiles is 4 out of 12, which is one in every three or $\frac{1}{3}$.

Two quantities are in **direct proportion** when they increase or decrease in the same ratio.

Example: If three drinks cost £1.20, what is the cost of 15 drinks?

This is five times the number of drinks, so it is five times the price.

£1.20 × 5 = £6

Practice activities

1. Look at these tile patterns. What proportion of each of the patterns is blue?

   a)

   _____

   b)

   _____

   c)

   _____

   d)

   _____

   e)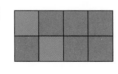

   _____

2. What is the ratio of blue to green tiles in the patterns in practice activity 1?

    a) ____ : ____   **b)** ____ : ____   **c)** ____ : ____

    d) ____ : ____   **e)** ____ : ____

3. Read and answer these.

    a) In a class there are two girls to every three boys.

         There are 30 children in the class. How many boys are there? ____

    b) A 200 g snack bar has 75% oats and 25% fruit.

         What is the ratio of oats to fruit in a bar, in its simplest form? ____ : ____

    c) Dan mixes 1 litre of white paint with every 4 litres of blue paint. He needs 30 litres of paint altogether.

         How many litres of blue paint will he need?   ____

4. In this recipe, the amount of each ingredient is given as a proportion of the total weight.

    a) Write the weights of each ingredient.

600 g Chocolate Chip Cookies	
$\frac{1}{2}$ flour	= ____ g
$\frac{1}{4}$ butter	= ____ g
$\frac{1}{6}$ sugar	= ____ g
$\frac{1}{12}$ chocolate chips	= ____ g

    b) Using this recipe, what weight of each ingredient would be needed for 900 g of cookies?

         flour = ____ g   butter = ____ g

         sugar = ____ g   chocolate chips = ____ g

Equations

Learn and revise

Equations have symbols or letters instead of numbers in a calculation.

$\Delta + 5 = 18$ $\qquad$ $4n - 2 = 18$ $\qquad$ $3y + 6 = 21$

Use the numbers given to help you work out the unknown symbol.

Example: $3y + 6 = 21$ $\qquad$ What is the value of y?

1. You want y on one side of the equation and the numbers on the other.

   Subtract 6 from both sides. If it was -6, you would add 6 to both sides.

   $3y = 21 - 6$ $\qquad$ $3y = 15$

2. Say the equation as a sentence: 3 times something makes 15.

   So $y = 5$.

3. Test it with the original equation: $3 \times 5 + 6 = 21$

Remember that equations need to stay balanced. If you add, take away, multiply or divide a number from one side, do the same to the other side and the equation stays the same.

Practice activities

1. Write the value of each symbol or letter.

   a) $15 + \Delta = 22$ $\qquad$ $\Delta = \underline{\hspace{1cm}}$

   b) $\blacklozenge - 9 = 6$ $\qquad$ $\blacklozenge = \underline{\hspace{1cm}}$

   c) $9 \times \blacklozenge = 18$ $\qquad$ $\blacklozenge = \underline{\hspace{1cm}}$

   d) $\blacklozenge \div 4 = 8$ $\qquad$ $\blacklozenge = \underline{\hspace{1cm}}$

   e) $y + 14 = 38$ $\qquad$ $y = \underline{\hspace{1cm}}$

   f) $20 - b = 15$ $\qquad$ $b = \underline{\hspace{1cm}}$

   g) $7n = 42$ $\qquad$ $n = \underline{\hspace{1cm}}$

   h) $27 \div t = 9$ $\qquad$ $t = \underline{\hspace{1cm}}$

2. Work out the value of each letter.

a) $5c + 8 = 28$ $c =$ _____

b) $4y - 16 = 4$ $y =$ _____

c) $18 + 3p = 30$ $p =$ _____

d) $2r + 5 = 23$ $r =$ _____

e) $7a - 11 = 10$ $a =$ _____

f) $4w + 9 = 49$ $w =$ _____

3. In an algebraic expression, letters are used as substitutes for numbers.
Find the value of the following expressions if $c = 5$ and $d = 8$.

a) $3c - d + 24 =$ _____

b) $34 + 5(d - c) =$ _____

c) $(84 - 4d) + (8c + 68) =$ _____

d) $2(d + c) - 7(d - c) =$ _____

e) $\dfrac{40}{d} - \dfrac{15}{c} =$ _____

f) $6(4c - 2d) + 6c =$ _____

4. The letters x and y stand for two whole numbers.

$xy = 24$

a) Which two numbers could x and y stand for? Write all the different
possibilities in pairs, e.g. [$x = ?, y = ?$]

_____

_____

b) What if $xy = 24$ and $x - y = 5$?

$x =$ _____

$y =$ _____

Mean, mode and median

Mode, **median** and **mean** are three types of average.

Example: This chart shows the goals scored by five players in a football team. What is the average for the number of goals scored?

Player	Alex	Billy	Chris	David	Eric
Goals scored	8	4	8	6	9

Mode: the most common number.

Two players scored **8** goals so that is the mode.

Median: the middle number when listed in order.

4, 6, **8**, 8, 9

So 8 is the median number of goals.

When there is an even number of items, the median is the midpoint between the **two** middle numbers.

Mean: add the numbers and divide the total by the number of items in the list.

4 + 6 + 8 + 8 + 9 = 35   35 ÷ 5 = 7

So the mean is 7 goals.

Practice activities

1. These are the results of a maths test out of 100 for a group of nine children:

    80   60   70   70   80   50   50   80   90

    a) Write the scores in order, starting with the highest.

    ___ ___ ___ ___ ___ ___ ___ ___ ___

    highest

    b) What is the median score?   ___

    c) Which score is the mode?   ___

    d) Calculate the mean score.   ___

2. These are the heights of a group of five children:

150 cm	140 cm	130 cm	140 cm	190 cm

   a) Which height is the mode?   _____ cm

   b) What is the median height?   _____ cm

   c) What is the mean height?   _____ cm

3. These are the times taken to run 200 metres by a group of athletes. What are the average times?

Name	Time (seconds)
Anna	28
Jo	34
Sally	29
Grace	28
Jasmine	31

Median: _____ seconds

Mode: _____ seconds

Mean: _____ seconds

4. These are the hand-spans for a group of 10 children.

   What are the average hand-spans for this group?

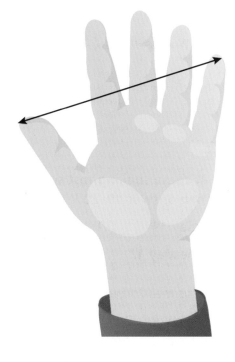

13 cm	11 cm
9 cm	10 cm
10 cm	8 cm
12 cm	9 cm
8 cm	10 cm

Median: _____ cm   Mode: _____ cm   Mean: _____ cm

Mental arithmetic test 11

1. $d + 54 = 72$

   $d =$ _____

   The ratio for making pastry is 1 : 2, butter to flour. Now answer 2–3.

2. If 50 g of butter is used, how much flour will be needed?

   _____ g

3. How much butter is needed if 400 g of flour is used?

   _____ g

4. Calculate this, when $p = 4$ and $m = 8$.

   $5m - 6p =$ _____

5. $8f = 56$

   $f =$ _____

   These are the numbers of children in each class in a school. Write the average class sizes in 6–8.

   | 32 | 28 | 29 | 28 | 33 |

6. Mode: _____

7. Mean: _____

8. Median: _____

9. What proportion of this pattern is red?

   _____

10. What is the ratio of red to white tiles above?

    _____ : _____

11. A 300 g apple pie is made with 75% apples and 25% pastry. What is the proportion of apples in the pie, in its simplest form?

    _____

12. $6t - 16 = 20$

    $t =$ _____

    These are the lengths of seven skipping ropes. Now answer 13–15.

    170 cm   165 cm   170 cm

    170 cm   190 cm   195 cm   165 cm

13. What is the median length? _____ cm

14. Which length is the mode? _____ cm

15. What is the mean length? _____ cm

16. If you buy eight pencils, you get a free sharpener. If a teacher buys 40 pencils, how many sharpeners will she get free?

    _____

17. Calculate this, when $j = 7$ and $k = 3$.

    $5(j - k) + 4j =$ _____

18. $25 + 7d = 46$

    $d =$ _____

    Look at these spelling test scores for Ross then answer 19–20.

    Monday 19   Tuesday 14

    Wednesday 17   Thursday 18

19. What is his mean score? _____

20. On Friday he got 12 in the spelling test. What is his mean score now?

    _____

Score   /20

50

Mental arithmetic test 12

1. What proportion of this pattern is red?

   _____

2. What is the ratio of red to white tiles above?

   _____ : _____

3. $42 \div z = 7$

   $z =$ _____

4. To make concrete two bags of cement are mixed with five bags of stones. If I use four bags of cement, how many bags of stones will I need?

   _____

   These are the weights of five apples. Use them to answer 5–7.

   32 g   35 g   34 g   32 g   37 g

5. Which weight is the mode? _____ g

6. What is the median weight? _____ g

7. What is the mean weight? _____ g

8. $10s = 200$

   $s =$ _____

9. There are four bread rolls in a bag and there are six cheese slices in a pack. I buy three bags of bread rolls. How many packs of cheese will I need for one slice of cheese for every bread roll?

   _____

10. Calculate this, when $c = 5$ and $d = 9$.

    $10c + 4d =$ _____

11. $3r + 12 = 30$

    $r =$ _____

12. A 400 ml carton has 25% juice and 75% water. What is the ratio of juice to water in the carton, in its simplest form?

    _____ : _____

13. $7y + 5 = 61$

    $y =$ _____

    These are the temperatures over one week in March. Write the average temperatures in 14–16.

15°C	**13°C**	**9°C**	**12°C**
	12°C	**12°C**	**11°C**

14. Mean: _____°C

15. Mode: _____°C

16. Median: _____°C

17. $9a - 5 = 22$

    $a =$ _____

18. Calculate this, when $v = 3$ and $w = 8$.

    $7(v + w) - 4v =$ _____

19. $zy = 21$. If $z = 7$, what is y?

    $y =$ _____

20. In a shoe shop they need to stock the size of shoe that sells the most. Would it be better to calculate the mean, mode or median average for this task?

    _____

Score   /20

Speed test

- How many of these can you complete correctly in one minute?
- Write your answers on paper. Number them 1 to 40.
- Don't worry if you cannot answer them all, just answer them as quickly as you can.
- Stop after one minute, check your answers and record your score on the progress chart opposite.
- Then, try again at another time to see if you can improve your score!

Addition and subtraction

1. 50 + 70 = _____

2. 19 + 8 = _____

3. 13 + 17 = _____

4. 0.9 – 0.2 = _____

5. 200 – 110 = _____

6. 15 + 16 = _____

7. 85 – 30 = _____

8. 19 + 7 = _____

9. 130 – 50 = _____

10. 60 – 8 = _____

11. 1200 – 300 = _____

12. 25 + 8 = _____

13. 1500 + 1500 = _____

14. $1\frac{2}{5} + \frac{1}{5}$ = _____

15. 60 + 80 = _____

16. 31 – 3 = _____

17. 450 + 500 = _____

18. 0.5 + 0.9 = _____

19. 18 – 9 = _____

20. 17 + 8 = _____

21. 200 + 900 = _____

22. 23 + 8 = _____

23. 13 – 6 = _____

24. 21 – 7 = _____

25. 0.6 + 0.7 = _____

26. 1.1 – 0.9 = _____

27. $\frac{1}{3} + \frac{1}{3}$ = _____

28. 16 – 8 = _____

29. 130 – 40 = _____

30. 17 – 11 = _____

31. 540 + 140 = _____

32. 170 + 80 = _____

33. $3\frac{4}{5} - \frac{3}{5}$ = _____

34. 19 + 6 = _____

35. 13 – 8 = _____

36. 280 + 50 = _____

37. 180 + 40 = _____

38. 0.8 – 0.5 = _____

39. 36 + 6 = _____

40. 110 – 70 = _____

Progress chart

Colour in the stars to show your correct answers.

Attempt	1	2	3	4	5	6
Date	....	....	....	....	....	....

Scores out of 40

Attempt 1	Attempt 2	Attempt 3	Attempt 4	Attempt 5	Attempt 6
39 40	39 40	39 40	39 40	39 40	39 40
37 38	37 38	37 38	37 38	37 38	37 38
35 36	35 36	35 36	35 36	35 36	35 36
33 34	33 34	33 34	33 34	33 34	33 34
31 32	31 32	31 32	31 32	31 32	31 32
29 30	29 30	29 30	29 30	29 30	29 30
27 28	27 28	27 28	27 28	27 28	27 28
25 26	25 26	25 26	25 26	25 26	25 26
23 24	23 24	23 24	23 24	23 24	23 24
21 22	21 22	21 22	21 22	21 22	21 22
19 20	19 20	19 20	19 20	19 20	19 20
17 18	17 18	17 18	17 18	17 18	17 18
15 16	15 16	15 16	15 16	15 16	15 16
13 14	13 14	13 14	13 14	13 14	13 14
11 12	11 12	11 12	11 12	11 12	11 12
9 10	9 10	9 10	9 10	9 10	9 10
7 8	7 8	7 8	7 8	7 8	7 8
5 6	5 6	5 6	5 6	5 6	5 6
3 4	3 4	3 4	3 4	3 4	3 4
1 2	1 2	1 2	1 2	1 2	1 2

Speed test

- How many of these can you complete correctly in one minute?
- Write your answers on paper. Number them 1 to 40.
- Don't worry if you cannot answer them all, just answer them as quickly as you can.
- Stop after one minute, check your answers and record your score on the progress chart opposite.
- Then, try again at another time to see if you can improve your score!

Multiplication and division

1. 6×12 = _____

2. 8×7 = _____

3. $99 \div 11$ = _____

4. $56 \div 8$ = _____

5. 8^2 = _____

6. 12×7 = _____

7. $36 \div 6$ = _____

8. $27 \div 3$ = _____

9. 400×2 = _____

10. $63 \div 9$ = _____

11. $100 \div 4$ = _____

12. 40×60 = _____

13. 2.1×10 = _____

14. $88 \div 8$ = _____

15. 0.2×7 = _____

16. 0.5×10 = _____

17. $1.8 \div 10$ = _____

18. $56 \div 7$ = _____

19. $42 \div 6$ = _____

20. 8×9 = _____

21. $60 \div 2$ = _____

22. 20×7 = _____

23. 11×11 = _____

24. $180 \div 3$ = _____

25. 3.45×100 = _____

26. 11×12 = _____

27. 30×9 = _____

28. 7^2 = _____

29. $19.8 \div 10$ = _____

30. $48 \div 8$ = _____

31. $54 \div 9$ = _____

32. 90×9 = _____

33. 2.3×10 = _____

34. 6^2 = _____

35. $600 \div 10$ = _____

36. $200 \div 4$ = _____

37. 2×800 = _____

38. 0.8×3 = _____

39. 90×7 = _____

40. $150 \div 5$ = _____

Colour in the stars to show your correct answers.

Attempt	1	2	3	4	5	6
Date						

Scores out of 40

1	2	3	4	5	6
39 40	39 40	39 40	39 40	39 40	39 40
37 38	37 38	37 38	37 38	37 38	37 38
35 36	35 36	35 36	35 36	35 36	35 36
33 34	33 34	33 34	33 34	33 34	33 34
31 32	31 32	31 32	31 32	31 32	31 32
29 30	29 30	29 30	29 30	29 30	29 30
27 28	27 28	27 28	27 28	27 28	27 28
25 26	25 26	25 26	25 26	25 26	25 26
23 24	23 24	23 24	23 24	23 24	23 24
21 22	21 22	21 22	21 22	21 22	21 22
19 20	19 20	19 20	19 20	19 20	19 20
17 18	17 18	17 18	17 18	17 18	17 18
15 16	15 16	15 16	15 16	15 16	15 16
13 14	13 14	13 14	13 14	13 14	13 14
11 12	11 12	11 12	11 12	11 12	11 12
9 10	9 10	9 10	9 10	9 10	9 10
7 8	7 8	7 8	7 8	7 8	7 8
5 6	5 6	5 6	5 6	5 6	5 6
3 4	3 4	3 4	3 4	3 4	3 4
1 2	1 2	1 2	1 2	1 2	1 2

Speed test

- How many of these can you complete correctly in one minute?
- Write your answers on paper. Number them 1 to 40.
- Don't worry if you cannot answer them all, just answer them as quickly as you can.
- Stop after one minute, check your answers and record your score on the progress chart opposite.
- Then, try again at another time to see if you can improve your score!

Mixed problems

1. 19 + 9 = _____

2. 80 + 60 = _____

3. 9 × 12 = _____

4. 400 − 30 = _____

5. 120 ÷ 2 = _____

6. 900 − 500 = _____

7. 36 ÷ 9 = _____

8. 70 + 40 = _____

9. 9 × 8 = _____

10. 121 ÷ 11 = _____

11. 22 − 7 = _____

12. 12 × 8 = _____

13. 1.5 − 0.6 = _____

14. 0.7 + 0.6 = _____

15. 500 + 500 = _____

16. 35 ÷ 7 = _____

17. 25 × 4 = _____

18. 110 − 30 = _____

19. 160 ÷ 4 = _____

20. 8 × 50 = _____

21. 30 × 6 = _____

22. 65 + 25 = _____

23. 180 ÷ 9 = _____

24. 22 − 5 = _____

25. 4^2 = _____

26. 23 + 8 = _____

27. 900 − 20 = _____

28. 700 × 5 = _____

29. 0.7 + 0.8 = _____

30. 18 + 20 = _____

31. 72 ÷ 6 = _____

32. 12 × 11 = _____

33. 24 − 5 = _____

34. 20 × 8 = _____

35. 56 ÷ 7 = _____

36. 120 ÷ 6 = _____

37. 80 ÷ 4 = _____

38. 120 − 40 = _____

39. 130 + 50 = _____

40. 12^2 = _____

Progress chart

Colour in the stars to show your correct answers.

Scores out of 40

Attempt	1	2	3	4	5	6
Date	....	....	....	....	....	....
	39 40	39 40	39 40	39 40	39 40	39 40
	37 38	37 38	37 38	37 38	37 38	37 38
	35 36	35 36	35 36	35 36	35 36	35 36
	33 34	33 34	33 34	33 34	33 34	33 34
	31 32	31 32	31 32	31 32	31 32	31 32
	29 30	29 30	29 30	29 30	29 30	29 30
	27 28	27 28	27 28	27 28	27 28	27 28
	25 26	25 26	25 26	25 26	25 26	25 26
	23 24	23 24	23 24	23 24	23 24	23 24
	21 22	21 22	21 22	21 22	21 22	21 22
	19 20	19 20	19 20	19 20	19 20	19 20
	17 18	17 18	17 18	17 18	17 18	17 18
	15 16	15 16	15 16	15 16	15 16	15 16
	13 14	13 14	13 14	13 14	13 14	13 14
	11 12	11 12	11 12	11 12	11 12	11 12
	9 10	9 10	9 10	9 10	9 10	9 10
	7 8	7 8	7 8	7 8	7 8	7 8
	5 6	5 6	5 6	5 6	5 6	5 6
	3 4	3 4	3 4	3 4	3 4	3 4
	1 2	1 2	1 2	1 2	1 2	1 2

Key facts

Multiplication and division facts

×	1	2	3	4	5	6	7	8	9	10	11	12
1	1	2	3	4	5	6	7	8	9	10	11	12
2	2	4	6	8	10	12	14	16	18	20	22	24
3	3	6	9	12	15	18	21	24	27	30	33	36
4	4	8	12	16	20	24	28	32	36	40	44	48
5	5	10	15	20	25	30	35	40	45	50	55	60
6	6	12	18	24	30	36	42	48	54	60	66	72
7	7	14	21	28	35	42	49	56	63	70	77	84
8	8	16	24	32	40	48	56	64	72	80	88	96
9	9	18	27	36	45	54	63	72	81	90	99	108
10	10	20	30	40	50	60	70	80	90	100	110	120
11	11	22	33	44	55	66	77	88	99	110	121	132
12	12	24	36	48	60	72	84	96	108	120	132	144

Decimal number system

Hundreds	Tens	Ones		Tenths	Hundredths	Thousandths
5	1	6	.	8	2	5
(500)	(10)	(6)		$\left(\frac{8}{10}\right)$	$\left(\frac{2}{100}\right)$	$\left(\frac{5}{1000}\right)$

516.825 is read as five hundred and sixteen point eight two five

Fractions, decimals and percentages

A fraction has two parts:

$\frac{2}{3}$ ⟵ numerator
⟵ denominator

Key facts

A **proper fraction** is less than 1. The numerator is smaller than the denominator, e.g. $\frac{3}{5}$	An **improper fraction** is greater than 1. The numerator is greater than the denominator, e.g. $\frac{5}{3}$	A **mixed number** is made up of a whole number and a fraction. $\frac{5}{3} = 1\frac{2}{3}$

Decimals	0.1	0.2	0.3	0.4	0.5	0.6	0.7	0.8	0.9	0.25	0.75
Fractions	$\frac{1}{10}$	$\frac{1}{5}$	$\frac{3}{10}$	$\frac{2}{5}$	$\frac{1}{2}$	$\frac{3}{5}$	$\frac{7}{10}$	$\frac{4}{5}$	$\frac{9}{10}$	$\frac{1}{4}$	$\frac{3}{4}$
Percentages	10%	20%	30%	40%	50%	60%	70%	80%	90%	25%	75%

Multiples

A multiple of a whole number is produced by multiplying that number by another whole number.

Multiples of 3 $\longrightarrow$ 3   6   9   **12**   15   18...   60...   300...

Multiples of 4 $\longrightarrow$ 4   8   **12**   16   20   24...   80...   400...

12 is the **lowest common multiple** (LCM) of 3 and 4.

Factors

The factors of 8 are **1**, **2**, **4** and **8**.

The factors of 24 are **1**, **2**, 3, **4**, 6, **8**, 12 and 24.

The factors of 32 are **1**, **2**, **4**, **8**, 16 and 32.

The common factors of 8, 24 and 32 are 1, 2, 4 and 8.

The **highest common factor** (HCF) of 8, 24 and 32 is 8.

Time

1 minute = 60 seconds

1 hour = 60 minutes

1 day = 24 hours

1 week = 7 days

1 fortnight = 14 days

1 year = 12 months = 365 days

leap year = 366 days

Acknowledgements

The author and publisher are grateful to the copyright holders for permission to use quoted materials and images.

P39 ©Julien Grondin; P39 ©Firtad; P45 ©Nataliia Natykach; P49 ©Natali Snailcat; P52, 54, 56 ©Elmm

The above images have been used under license from Shutterstock.com

All other images are ©Jupiterimages, ©Thinkstock or ©Letts Educational, an imprint of HarperCollins*Publishers* Ltd

Every effort has been made to trace copyright holders and obtain their permission for the use of copyright material. The author and publisher will gladly receive information enabling them to rectify any error or omission in subsequent editions. All facts are correct at time of going to press.

Published by Letts Educational
An imprint of HarperCollins*Publishers* Ltd
1 London Bridge Street
London SE1 9GF

ISBN 9781844198634

First published 2013

This edition published 2015

10 9 8 7 6 5 4 3 2 1

Text © 2015 Paul Broadbent

Design © 2015 Letts Educational, an imprint of HarperCollins*Publishers* Ltd

The author asserts his moral right to be identified as the author of this work.

British Library Cataloguing in Publication Data.

A CIP record of this book is available from the British Library.

Commissioning Editor: Tammy Poggo

Author: Paul Broadbent

Project Manager: Richard Toms

Editorial: Amanda Dickson, Richard Toms and Marie Taylor

Cover Design: Sarah Duxbury

Inside Concept Design: Ian Wrigley

Layout: Jouve India Private Limited

Printed and bound by RR Donnelley APS